THE LAUGHTER OF ADAM AND EVE

CRAB ORCHARD SERIES IN POETRY

Open Competition Award

THE LAUGHTER OF ADAM AND EVE

POEMS BY JASON SOMMER

Crab Orchard Review &
Southern Illinois University Press
Carbondale

16 15 14 13   4 3 2 1

The Crab Orchard Series in Poetry is a joint publishing venture
of Southern Illinois University Press and *Crab Orchard Review.*
This series has been made possible by the generous support of the
Office of the President of Southern Illinois University and the
Office of the Vice Chancellor for Academic Affairs and Provost at
Southern Illinois University Carbondale.

Editor of the Crab Orchard Series in Poetry: Jon Tribble
Judge for the 2012 Open Competition Award: Cynthia Huntington

Library of Congress Cataloging-in-Publication Data
Sommer, Jason.
[Poems. Selections]
The laughter of Adam and Eve : poems / by Jason Sommer.
pages ; cm. — (Crab Orchard series in poetry)
ISBN-13: 978-0-8093-3278-6 (pbk. : alk. paper)
ISBN-10: 0-8093-3278-7 (pbk. : alk. paper)
ISBN-13: 978-0-8093-3279-3 (ebook)
ISBN-10: 0-8093-3279-5 (ebook)
I. Title.
PS3569.O6532L38 2013
811'.54—dc23   2013008339

Printed on recycled paper. ♻
The paper used in this publication meets the minimum requirements
of American National Standard for Information
Sciences—Permanence of Paper for Printed Library Materials,
ANSI Z39.48-1992. ∞

for Allison,

for Gabriel

CONTENTS

Acknowledgments

Grateful acknowledgment is made to the periodicals in which these poems first appeared:

AGNI ONLINE: "Brouhaha"

Boulevard: "Resignation Bird," "Signs and Wonders," "Film Clips of Munkacs, 1933"

Crab Orchard Review: "The One Who Knows All Language"

Delmar: "First Things"

Sou'wester: "The Laughter of Adam and Eve: A Detail"

The Cincinnati Review: "New Covenant, Causality," "Passengers Will . . . ," "Gunga Din," "No Script"

The Cortland Review: "Escaped to Tell"

Witness: "Plague Tale"

Thanks also to *Poetry Daily* for posting "The Laughter of Adam and Eve: A Detail."

I want to express my deep appreciation to my first responders—Alan Shapiro, Jane O. Wayne, Chuck Sweetman, Shane Seely, Jeff Hamilton, Lisa Ampleman, and Lisa Pepper—for their help and encouragement, and to thank Cynthia Huntington for her selection of my manuscript and Jon Tribble for his attentive reading of it.

THE LAUGHTER OF ADAM AND EVE

The Laughter of Adam and Eve: A Detail

As has been established in Midrash
elsewhere, the first hilarity in the world
occurred as they were making their way east
along one of the branches of the river Nod
in a near-desert place: ochre dust-
devils and shale, scrub grass and the sun
whirling light down as off the flat
of that sword burning behind them,
                              and Adam
struck with a kind of fit, shaking and stamping,
doubling over, rocking back, hinging, unhinging,
making sounds he could only have gotten
from the beasts of the field—
over what?
                 She doesn't quite know and yet
she starts to get it, take it from him,
him up from a bow with his head
thrown back, the whatsit stuck
midway in his craw now bobbing
interestingly—almost before she sees
her belly gives some sympathetic twitches

as *etz* he says to her in the original, *etz*
tree, tree, gasping this,
                        what the scrawny
item baking on the banks
turned out to be on inspection.
So pathetic a thing it was compared
to those majesties that knowledge
first depended from, and life:
all green hands turning, over
and back, light side, dark side,
slatting a glimpse of the red suns
of the fruit—
                all green wings rising, banking,

stalling aquiver with God's garden
wind, unseeable but good,
ambling about in the heat of the day,
all green tongues whispering where are you?
What have you done?

Tree?

This thing? And she lets go
to the sky in her pitches higher than his,
birds of the air more like, then to him,
a rough breathing, a half a voice,
an almost nothing itself to be closing
and opening the jaws on.
The curse notwithstanding,
this first fruit of exile he offers her,
plucked bodily but with some ease
from the barren land, is sustenance forever:
a knowledge of evil that is good.

New Covenant, Causality

In the beginning now no longer, what happens
happens for reasons, leaving spoor behind
as if a wounded beast had crashed through brush.

Sometimes the trail is as hard to follow as when
the hundred-year oak felled by a windstorm
lay in the sun for days, the uprooted end

a pried-up cache of antler and tusk, and in
the midst thereof, strings, too, tethering into
the pit where the farmer's girl and boy played

until the tremble into motion, swinging
shut the lid to the gouged earth as the tree
righted, killing the children. The inquiry then

desperate, so as not to blame the father
alone who harvested some of the splayed limbs,
and a section also of counterweighing crown

so that, dismembered and topped, the trunk's repose
was flexion, bowed or arched-back struggle
to stand on what still branched underground.

Blame, though, must be apportioned, objects accused,
the usual laws of nature brought to account,
but after the death of innocence by the garden

tree from which knowledge hung, and in the cool
of days since, when the motive of everything
disguises itself in blankness, call it again

a species of wind, even if there were none,
the smallest breath of ever-moving air
over the face of the water, the principal light

burning by day down, evaporation
tautening then the most tendrilous roots
until the old tree rose up in the presence.

THE ONE WHO KNOWS ALL LANGUAGE

To one who knows all languages
no human-authored sound means nothing

and even words that mean precisely
nothing in every tongue are laden

with an intent beneath intention—
are laden, and he lades beyond

the easy cognates of a near
relation, ears flitting him like a pair

of wings, Ur to Cochin, Sarawak
to Hangzhou in a single sentence.

Here, with him, the false alarms
of homonym ring true elsewhere

or antonym with synonym
will fuse then part. Each phoneme is

like a germ is to disease full blown,
as twinge is to agony. He smiles

at something very like an "O"
of exhalation that at other

times has made him weep outright.
It never is a mistake, though, even

occasions when he sees the speakers'
faces and will take love for hate.

No one escapes his understanding.
He knows the hand signs, and also how

they may be pressed into the palm.
For years he'd try to make them hear

what he does so they'd admire his hearing.
But no more explanations now.

He eavesdrops only, deeper than
the personal, the hackneyed seven

secrets anyone might have,
in favor of sororal and

fraternal melody—he hears
and overhears, attends and listens

to the music of the common
origin, past Babel into Eden.

BROUHAHA

is the Jew, the dark Jews
present in you,
in your very mouth
unbeknownst.
Brouhaha you say after
them, long after
the despised, and so now
in their honor,
from the Hebrew of—

so scholars say, by way
of French—
barukh ha-ba,
blessed be the one who arrives,
said in a tumble of voices,
a crowd chorusing
the repeated phrase,
barukh ha-ba,
greeting the one who does

enter among them,
a caftaned traveler
who comes with news for those
gathered in the narrow courtyard,
spilling into the street,
the wave of greeting passing
through them in an untidy mix
of voices lapping over one another.
What sounds like nonsense

to the gentile passerby
with business in the quarter—
everyone speaking at once
if not quite together,
all that tribe,

heard as from a height
in clamorous babble,
except something emerges,
almost a word—

garble the stranger overhears
as *brouhaha*,
thinks to store for mockery,
and passes it along till somehow
it becomes the devil's
cry as he arrives on stage
circa 1490 in *Farce*
de Martin de Cambray
(or rather it is an actor playing

the horny priest disguised
as the devil sounding
like a Jew apparently—
who knew? Did the audience
know the sound of a Jew when
they heard it?).
A word from words
unmooring from what they meant,
drifting to something else,

become a word commotion
gave itself out of the confusion
of the tribes—things to speak of,
things to say, however
they arrive, say after me:
blessed be the arrival of that
which brings to the tongue
taste, and sustenance to the body
of our speech.

AT THE AKHMATOVA MUSEUM, FOUNTAIN HOUSE ANNEX

Eleven people knew Requiem *by heart and not one of them betrayed me.*

In her room where I stood so many years
later: two figures only
at a time back then,

and the word above all.

The woman with the strong line of
profile—there is a charcoal of her here in aquiline
silhouette, in soft hat, portraited after
the portraits of Dante—

she is mouthing the words over and over
to the other

woman who silently repeats: a line,
several at a time,
whole stanzas, both pouring

over the paper at intervals, and then without it again,

between the bursts of inconsequential
conversation: *how early autumn came this year!*

Not daring even the whisper
practiced waiting on line
for hours outside Kresty Prison,
the parcel in hand that if the warders
take means the prisoner is alive—
there may be listeners anywhere.

In the little room, just once or twice
drawn close to one another,
one breathes into the ear
of the other who breathes back again.

If it is winter, there is a fire
in the tall white stove
flowing around the logs
washing them away.

The tall, pale woman
who made the poem looks
at the shape of the poem she made
on her friend's lips. The hours
of the making,
the hours of the learning

off by heart, and the moment
would come. The visitor
has the poem now,

and the writer takes the paper,
opening the iron door of the stove,
slipping it onto the fire,

and the two watch
the paper seized by the flames
convulse against a log.

Or if there were no fire,
Akhmatova would make
a small one in an ash tray

and Chukovskaya would leave
with what she had to declare

mouth to ear, to paper again
someday, reassembling the requiem,
assembling us around it,

mouth and ear and mind's eye.

She moves down Liteyny Prospect
with no outward sign of having

what she has,
nothing to alert those who
might be watching
that anything had changed.

Signs and Wonders

The woman with the hair he thought like braided
bread, like challah, chains of it atop her head
the first he saw of her as he whisked through
the channels, turns out to be from Jews, a father's
father or so converted to some version of enthusiastic
Christianity, if not precisely hers. (He has seen what he has seen
on television—the rest he read.)

She weeps a lot. He has caught her in tears often
as he intended only to pass her program by
but stopped fascinated by such virtuosa
shedding and by the copious retentions
in the feathers or folds of that hairdo (no braids since,
maybe he was wrong about that), which seems out of time
in several ways—cruelly forgivable in someone younger,
a country music star onstage at the Grand
Ole Opry in 1958—a wig of course, wigs,
sometimes as gold as challah, the light on the crust
or the eggy insides, other tints, too, the pink
of pink champagne. Her tears have been for children
in the tropics to whom she sends dolls dressed as frilly
as she does but whose hair merely attempts plausibility.

One insomniac night he gives up the book
and goes downstairs to take up the remote control,
climbing through finally to the higher
stations, lingering for a story from her childhood
about their playing in the yard with a chicken—the playmate
a sister perhaps, she and another anyway, at play
as many oh many's the time before. The audience
listen rapt as the camera moves over them, such fixity of face—
he puts it down to discomfort with being watched—
but they must have come to be there in that studio then because of her
and hear now the way the girls become distracted by something
across the way. They leave the yard with the gate ajar—as children
will, she says, getting the "wi" like a "wh" is supposed to be,
it strikes him, if he remembers rightly
the pronunciation, definite as penmanship,
teachers passed on without practicing themselves.

The children cross the road onward to whatever had drawn
them, he doesn't think she specified, unaware the chicken followed
in time for a passing car to swat and grind it down into the roadbed's
dirt or tar, until the children hear the sound and turn.
She trembles with new tears, moved at the memory of the old
occasion: the bird a twisted duster, a fan
of feather and blood, an eye dangling down beside the broken
beak. She says she had seen her daddy, who was, you know,
a minister of the Lord, in his anointing in the spirit
and so she lay on her hands, weeping freely now as she wept,
cradling the chicken then and praying: Oh father and Oh heavenly king.

Again the camera sweeps and still he can't tell what anybody thinks
who sits in the seats across from the kitsch grandeur
of the set, living room cum throne room.
He's seen, he's sure he's seen, audiences in motion,
full of nodding assent, and sway, and cries, and amens,
on their feet, hands tilted up for what descends,
or a sign that it's descending, teary eyes skyward or fixed on the stage.
This bunch, though, deacon-solemn, dead still,
and when the camera settles on one man for a moment
at the end of a row, does he discern in that face a fearfulness
of anticipation as she goes on to where she had been going?
She tells how she looks down and sees the undoing
undone: the outted eye socketed, beak-crack
mended, blood back inside, and, set down, the chicken
jerking up and into its head-bobbing walk.

When he speaks about what he has witnessed—
a few weeks later, a sort of party piece at a gathering
of university friends and colleagues, showing off his mimicry—
he refers to it as the story of the resurrected
chicken only after he reaches the point where
it is revived, not to spoil the surprise for
his sophisticated listeners. She never actually said
it was dead, however, he's about to stress again
when his friend Jerry breaks in to accuse him
of suspect obsession, of getting to know entirely too much
about these charlatans, lunatics who brought down upon us
George W. Bush and the plague of idiots and murders besides,
to whom God also whispers, places things
in their hearts as if they were drop boxes for divine
instruction. What do you really want with them anyway?

What does he want? With them? I want, he says,
I really want, my mother to lean her poor emptying head
against the television screen and, laved in the prickly static,
to rock back and rise up healed
remembering who everybody is. I want to know
not if but that I have a soul, or something like,
a permanent part and suitable for cosmic travel.
And for the armies—

World peace, Jerry says, if I should win
Miss America I will work for—

—Well, shit yes, and I'm not certain I can explain
this very well, but I want the woman
with the hair not to have been conscious she hadn't
mentioned the chicken's death outright but truly to believe
she brought it back, and I want my countryman
in the close-up in the studio, and the others, too, to have their doubts.

Film Clips of Munkacs, 1933

These bits of film are all the light
left to us of the tens of thousands
come to Munkacs for the Rebbe's
daughter's wedding,
                    reflecting like moons,
worlds, each of them. Jews
in sashes in bicycle parade,
or massed, adrift, crossing the field
of view on foot: fedoras, shtreimels,
marriage wigs and kerchiefs, one white
babushka, long coats, dark coats, coats
of many colors in monochrome,
faces bespectacled or not
as can be seen, feet shod as can't—

all such as will be the harvest of
other light than this that fixes
them a solid phalanx framed
on screen awaiting the wedding party,
several thousand with their million
tiny movements like the blink
of leaves in the first hard scattering
of rain—small startlements
in the general sway of limb that presses
bodies against the straining line
of gendarmes, high helmets bobbing,
and the white babushka again, against
them down right, drawing the eye.

If it's true that light goes on forever,
could some of what these people reflect
pass by the sun it came from, continue
outward into the universe
to be received there just as we
here, looking on the countenance
of stars, receive the images
of icy calm or fierce last gasping
that traveled eons to us in silence?

It's sound that dies at the air's border.
His voice remains with us only,
the Munkatcher Rebbe, tightly ringed
in an eddy of crowd, speechifying
through microphones to America,
finger-wagging to remember
the Sabbath to keep it holy which many
have not forgotten but do not keep,
cannot keep instead, of course,
much of these figures at the wedding:

a glimpse of the bride making her way
to the synagogue, but broad backs
of Hassids in their striped black serge
and a flash photographer in the khaki
and cap of a soldier smother the Chuppah
scene and therefore have become it.
Beyond them from a space at the center
chanted blessings rise to disperse
in air like smoke.

We can't be sure
we've seen the groom whose history
is of the lesser agonies
even direct sun does little
to illuminate. He will survive
to renounce the post inherited
at the famous father-in-law's death.
He will accept, at least enough
to live in their state, the Zionists
he and his father-in-law so
inveighed against,
                    these very ones
who dance—young men and women linking
hands to step the steps of Hora
in two concentric circles, and one
smaller ring beside, round
and round as if for the Hassid wedding,
but if so it's so in counter joy
that the worlds might know another sort
than thou-shalt-not and next-world Hassids.
They sing and wheel, dancing to
the verses they sing over and over.

The song two-hundred-something children
sing once through in their filmed moments
is Hatikvah, which the old Rebbe would
have condemned—if not the *kinder* themselves,
then that desire the girls and boys
are taught to sing with the song, to have
the land before the Messiah comes.
Some few of them—star faces, faces
angled every phase of moon—
may have reached that land. The light could show.

Gunga Din

A sudden formal turn, the last hours
of a visit, my father calls me in to sit
across from him and asks that if I write
again from stories he's told me would I honor
the memory of the man who carried water
for their detachment of slave-laborers
who fed scrap into the hell's mouth smelter—
like something out of Dante—anyway,
did I remember what he'd told me about
that faithful man, my father wants to know?

I remembered that he hadn't so much told
me as I'd been allowed to overhear
since he knew better than to speak to me
directly then, into the adolescent
fumarole I iced over in irony,
my constant mode with him as much as I dared—
to guard against my tendency to believe—
and wound him when I could for things that I
was given to remember without prompt,
the times he'd roared and struck, the heavy-handed
absences, the stories of privation
depriving me, locked in with him inside
that closed economy with almost all
the space for story taken, and still more room
required to have his life squeeze through again
and again some narrow passage to survival.
I believed him a type of deceiver, charmer, at least
of others, which seemed the equivalent to me,
who believed I'd seen his truest face in rage.
Jealousy also whatever else it was.

I listened closely then, though, from the edge
of audience—New Rochelle, new people, all
except my mother and me—a lawyer's house,
the open-plan downstairs our whole Bronx
apartment would have fit into twice over:
my father's head-waggle signifies
modesty. For himself, he claims just luck,
although he sometimes calls it providence,
but virtue for the little man who humped
the buckets, a yoke made of his own bowed
shoulders, stiffened arms, on a stooping scurry
of a run from the pump, and running always, one
thing shining in his head: to do, do—
water for thirsty brothers—this to do
and done well all may yet be well. Ferrying
into the circle of the smelter's heat,
he waits for the men who serve the molten roiling:
lifting together rafts of checker plate,
engine casings, lengths of rail, pieces
of locomotive wheels. Anyone's slacking
a moment, or stumble, might mean deadfall of iron
on everyone. The motherly smile he offers
each with the ladle, as if he had prepared
a meal—in this, too, as in his frantic service,
he's made to seem to me idiotic.

My father says he never knew the man's
real name. They always called him Gunga Din
out of that crazy film inflated from
the Kipling poem, where Sam Jaffe, Sam
pretty, *yaffe* the Hebrew for it, pock-marked
simian Jew plays Indian, Hindu or Sikh,
as Jews played cavalry-fodder Indians
in Westerns—other, other, their faces merely
other, and once other they might be any
kind of other; and this man other to
my father surely and to his fellow slaves:
a simpleton reduced to that simple thing,
as selfless as if he understood he was
and assented to being a minor character
in someone else's story. Amid hard labor,
the harder labor of the rest, no matter
how hard he'd made his own, wouldn't he be
a comic figure often, the butt of jokes,
water boy in the company of men?

Wasn't the name itself a sort of joke?
I ask my father what I'd always thought.
No no, he says, we loved him, drawing himself
up and back in his chair, looking at me
surprised, and I see for the moment I believe
him what he means for me to see: a whole
world beyond irony, full of unintricate
acts, and love there simple as slaked thirst.

SAINT KEVIN, BLACKBIRD, AND OTHERS

And since the whole thing's imagined anyhow,
Imagine being Kevin. Which is he?
Self-forgetful or in agony all the time . . .

—Seamus Heaney

I'll take my version of the fiction this way,
a moment of the natural man beforehand:
St. Kevin as the patron of the morning
yawn and stretch, his arms our-lord-extended-
cruciform to unkink after the cramped
night in the booth. Because that's what it is,
pallet-narrow if not quite pallet-long
enough, cockpit of prayer, the true-to-life
of medieval illuminations in which
lords wear their tiny castles like a costume
in the columns of a vellum manuscript.
I visualize the hermit with both arms
out windows, either side, into the green.

Palms up, knees down, begin the orisons—
right then, while he's not yet in full immersion,
I'd have it happen. Sound and feel at once
of one hand clapping, blurred applause of wings
on the left, and twiggy claw-scratch, warm heft
jouncing, the heart's trill—hers—the blackbird lights,
straw in mouth, egg in arse, deposits
both for starters in the little space
of several wingbeats, sets to her brooding, bird
in the hand's hollow.
                    Next flutter is his,
Kevin's, God's man in nature and above it—
on the evidence of other tales—as when
the willow trees give apples, water turns
to beer—beasts, too, his to command who is
commanded now himself.

                    Something beyond
and in him, through him, has him certain he
will never stir until the hatchlings go
nestlings, go fledglings, are gone from the hand
frozen in proffer pose over the sill,
a reflex to immobility like the one
to motion that grips the passerby who runs
into the burning building for the stranger
as urgently as if that life's his own.

My father was an acrobat of stillness
once, but only for his own sake, the time
he tells about—escaped from labor camp,
no room for him to hide with Naiman Imre
as they'd arranged. Instead, he's penned beneath
the stairs of a Budapest apartment house
for days, in terror that the least scrape
of sound would summon those who'd turn him in—
till thirst and hunger drive him to risk the street.

In the boxcar, my Aunt Lilly can make no movement
of her own. Bodies of others hold her still,
even the dead kept upright in the shaking
till Birkenau, where, nights, the living, bone
to bone, will cram, four to a plank bunk.
She has a way with her starvation, though,
Sundays behind the barracks with her sisters,
dreaming up banquet menus, forshpeis to sweet:
kreplach in soup—then, brisket, or sturgeon—
maybe a goose. Tzimmes on the side;
to finish: shlishkes, compote, and honey cake—
abstracted longing sharper than the hunger,
apparently. Still, how must that have felt?
Fever visions then, retold now calmly?

I know that it must seem I'm trumping myth
with history, Seamus, *il miglior fabbro*.
I intend you no corrective, especially
not the sort survivors will administer
by right and often simply by their tone
addressing those who've had the privilege
of afterwards and elsewhere, luxurious
Americans, children even when they're grown.
These children, theirs or others, ask their stories,
attracted to extremity as to
a laboratory of the true, as if
out far enough, or down toward human zero—
till there was nowhere further must be truth.
Trying to imagine, still I go
through Lilly and my father at their limit
to get to Kevin Zen, either so mindful
he's disembodied, or else saintly contorted,
weeks in the martyrdom of itch and ache,
the store of anguish inexhaustible
and open all hours.
                              Of course, my father and aunt
are in no seizure of universal love—
these episodes or a hundred others, worse—
no holy spirit, graceless, untranscending.
Despite my father's saying he'd been spared
by God, there hadn't been a sign of it
as things unfolded, beyond survival itself.
At home from college when he came out with that
in company around the table, I smoldered
for hours until I got a chance outside
alone with him to hiss my righteous anger
for the murdered others. What was the logic here?
God so loved him and hated all the rest?

Of suffering they seemed to know only
that they had suffered, not for the faith, for nothing
really, and from that nothing, not much to say,
even prompted, of how they managed it.
In fear, in pain, in ceaseless calculation
over thin soup and ersatz bread, in thirst
in hunger, in—entirely in—these were
the states of being they would answer with.
But was there anything else? Not respite merely,
a lull in threat or the grinding labor over
for awhile, but rather inside each, gaps
where the spirit nests and senses in the midst
of all that happens almost nothing moving?

Kevin, using his free hand, can reach
larder and cistern—pine nuts, dried fruit, apples
in any season, and small rain from the heavens.
He finds a way to flex the other arm,
has packed grass between it and the sill,
can shift enough not to shake out what's in
the nest and still have blood go round its round—
less about the body game ascetics play,
then, more the middle path. Sometimes it is
the petty body's turn; sometimes self
utterly recedes. It's the ordinary
alternations the mercy's in—attention,
inattention, the trance of minuscule distractions,
concentration elsewhere—ants at portage
under burdens larger than themselves
trail past. The webs that break across his face
are the mist that burns off the lough all through the morning.
Fugue states shine their countenance upon
now and at the hour amen selah.
A scant month and a half, and empty-handed,
blackbirds up and gone, the nest's debris
tipped from the palm onto the turfy ground.

No Script

In the midst, improvised,
no script but the one we are writing,
my mother and I,
a scene utterly without dialogue
in an old story.

They are in their pull-out sofa bed, green Castro
Convertible, in the living room—
I have the bedroom in this one-bedroom
apartment—my father is asleep beside her. I climb in
on her side of the bed, press in at her back and throw
a leg over her hips and she pushes
my leg off—once, twice, then hard,
but without speaking. And the scene goes away,
or I go away from it, back to my room
perhaps; anyway, what is marked for memory concludes
with me in their bed.

Nothing much had happened, and
except that it is
a story of the sort it is, except the sharpness
of the bewilderment and hurt, not much to remember.

*

She might have said something, but didn't.
What could she have said to make either of us
at ease with what we did and did not
understand? We were moving through our lives
that morning, newly awake or awakened,
surely less than half asleep, though unable to say
words, neither the four- or five-year-old
boy nor the twenty-seven- or twenty-eight-
year-old woman, coming to those moments:
our little variations of the stories
in their constellations, familiar, navigable—
at least to return by.

*

Was anything of her silence for my father?
Had she been afraid of wakening him?
Troubled sleeper sleeping then,
mound on the other side of her, hardly stirring,
not quite a shape in the curtained dark.
Awake, awakened he has bellowed before.
I don't remember if he had yet snaked out
his belt from the loops.
Him flailing at me, me on my back on the bed,
my legs up in defense, thighs to chest,
in that other room, she in the doorway,
saying his name several times over, too softly.

*

Shouldn't she have known—a college-educated woman—
so that we wouldn't fail at a chance
of some necessary realignment?
What I wanted, appeared to want, slipping into the bed
I could not have wanted—
couldn't have known to want.
Ridiculous to think the failure was right then,
just then. Hers must be the failure, I am innocent
by most conventions.

*

She'd read for me: those rhymes,
"The Pobble Who Has No Toes,"
and later, "I'm Nobody! Who Are You?"
I read because of her, and spoke,
although I can't remember
the way she brought me out of infancy
to language, I've seen her with my children,
babies held eye to eye, when they could barely
make a sound that wasn't signal of the body's needs.
She'd answer any sound of theirs
with words, a "yes," first,
and then tell them what they were trying
to say, what they looked as if they said, all melody
and ending on that lilt which was
an invitation to reply, a promise
she would reply again, which she did for hours.
They almost seemed to speak, got the form
of speech then, taking their turn
at babble. Until, the time, years on, they spoke to her
too freely, and she simply turned away, barely spoke
and, when she had to, censure hummed
beneath everything, just in the range of hearing.

*

At fifteen, at seventeen,
at twenty—the stories, the true story
of young women,
who had turned away
from me with no reason.

The causal part was blank
mystery. Suddenly they turned
and that was all,

and into their refusal
even to speak about it anymore,
I would speak, send words—
letters, lines—words on words,
set down on paper, sent

and then unsent after a while,
spoken into the air,
set down in notebooks.
How could she not return
for those words?—
even if they chided a little,

words of as much beauty as
I could manage and
about beauty:
the way the beautiful are

seldom eager, staring out
purblindly into the fog
where the rest of us, in our
unseemly straining forward,
offer to change ourselves
into something beauty
might want—and me among them,
asking her to believe
I was the only one who could
tell her these things.
Wouldn't she have to answer
with her return?

Resignation Bird

Not quite dawn but already
three notes descending
to middle C, mi re doh
doh doh, a three times
bounce of the last,

the birdsong I hear as
I'll make do do do,
whatever the bird sings—
the resignation bird,
whichever the bird.
Some resolve, though,
in the words. You could
hear that in their sound.

I've felt the way a whistling
can drill directly for
the spirit, the high liquids
of a canary, but this
is fluted, breathy, breathed
across the opening
of the garden.

I believed it was nearly gone,
my desire that every song
have words, the impulse to
supply them, to tell
what's sung, say while singing,
but there is still this
vestige again now that
day has come come come.

Sleeping with a Woman Who Writes

To M. Maloney

Which is what you have done.
Not a novelist, dangerous enough,
but a diarist, a nonprofessional
who disseminated her account electronically
among friends who did some distributing of
their own, maybe as much for the lively
writing as for the stunning
frankness—

        and so I know the size
of your member, its roseate, marmoreal
shine erect; the fact that you owned up
to having a wank earlier in the day
you were due to sleep with her for
a second time—hard to say, though,
from the context why you confided that;
the postcoital compliment, fairly laden
in too many ways, that she would have earned
a Porsche by her performance, a reference
to your earlier conversation about the virtues
of expensive cars, but clumsy, clumsy!

Of course she hyped romance up from the first
encounter at the bar, in time
with the hectic drumming, in tune
with your soulful lead guitar—some way out

for however long you'd be in town
of her morass, or worse a way to go that round
of hers of generally believing she's not good
enough, and specifically not good enough
for someone glamorous as you seemed,
so she enacts a fumbling ungoodness
sufficient to have it confirmed.
Yes, yes, she had momentum
before she got to you, and so did you:
luxuria of the traveling man, seed-scatterer,
fingerer of keyboards as well as strings, also.

If she hadn't kept her diary
from you—this data entry that she does
outside of work to tend her melancholy—
if you hadn't added to her melancholy—
whatever else you might have avoided,
surely you would not have pillow-talked,
in the first night's trade of confidences,
about your child with the bipolar girl
back home you signed away all rights to
(no road liaison—you simply never
have them)—then asking her, this unknown
writer there in bed with you, for reassurance
that she wasn't mad as well. To which she replied
she thought that many people were,
if only just a smidge.

All these trespasses against the privacy
of the personal life, notwithstanding,
she comes off all right, despite the insecurities
and silliness and babble, as persuasive
of truthfulness as a good poem of a certain sort.
You, however, your clear connivance
with bandmates not to be alone with her at dinner
after the night she got drunk and went on
an ecological rant over how you'd dumped
those batteries, and your two-bit psychologizing
early on: your control of where
your thoughts go; there are techniques
that she could learn to make herself
less anxious. Lastly, that dream you told her
meant she really wanted to be a free-
roaming Appaloosa mare; interpretation
as maneuver before the phoned excuses.

She sees that she's been had,
has been a bit much in her usual mode
of being that, penance to follow
the written confession, but she also sees
what other women have seen one by one
in the old slow sequential ways
and will now with the new rapidity,
how you couldn't please even if
you wanted to, no traction as she puts it; that is,
what a tiny prick you are in every way.

The Love of Pygmalion

You can't do anything that I could not
imagine you would do, and I was tired
already of myself, hence you, and hence
your face, so featured, breasts depending so,
ankles tapered, all to my design,

each element selected out of what
I'd seen, material to make the unseen
visible: golden ratios to figure
into limb and trunk, particulars I mused
on, street and marketplace: the slender turn

of a wrist, or maybe something sturdier,
the buoyant curls of hair, or waves or straight
fall of the black or fair or red . . . or . . . or . . .
No sooner had I planned for any aspect
one kind of beauty than I conceived another,

and came back round to my first thought, circling
for instance several times the same few answers
to the question of your neck—whatever troubled,
what could decide me ever, stalled often
at the swinging gate of either this or that?

Dilemma come down to hips, I glimpsed choice's
circuitry: if they were wide they'd be as wide
as those I'd sat astride in infancy,
if narrow, narrow as mine had been as a boy.
Oh, how the goddess struck and struck—and struck,

I worshipped where I'd merely engineered
perfection, at the mounds and in the grotto
of difference, desperate that you be counterpart
and other, and other more perfectly than any
other could be. Then Venus unrelenting,

even in mercy presumptive, brought you to life,
where differences weren't differences enough
to rescue me. Your lips' first trembling smile,
déjà vu as on the moving face
of water: the scene a pool at which I see

myself almost as someone else who gazes
down on one whom he thinks someone else
but isn't, so dives in to love himself.
If by some vivifying miracle
again, such acts had issue, you'd be it.

LOVER

He mounts a kind of quest
beginning at the breast
to discover what he lost,

returning to those sites
recalling never quite
recovers from the light

gleaming off the sheets,
but the heartbeat and the heat
and the staring until sleep,

eyes locked onto eyes,
give him what he desires
more than otherwise.

A as Insignia

1.

If this were battle
it would be studied
for its own sake, to observe
the behavior of comrade-
combatants and not for how
it affected the outcome of a war.

2.

She tried not to think *narrow
shoulders.*
Her hips were more boyish than he liked.
Neither could stand the curtains in the room
but only lived with them for hours
at a time.
The whole apartment was provisional as a tent,
a flat which might be taken down
at any time, signs of habitation meant
to hearten or deceive.

3.

In the trenches not every touch
had nuance. There was simply comfort
in them
in the face of danger.

4.

Evading capture, there
they could tell the truth quietly
without consequence, without
it becoming part or alteration of
the current of a life.

5.

In code: a secret analog
for a secret self,
as much that as contempt
for all the ordinary
command structures of a life,
nakedness then, an analog
for intimacy, but also uniform
and disguise for.

6.

Meeting by a plan of time
and place.

7.

Whole civilizations
go on elsewhere.
The mission is to skirt the parallel
world, to meander
through the jungle or
to spend a few hours in the clearing,

a wandering apparently aimless,
a purposeful keeping still

by which information is gathered,
minor intelligence.

8.

As if to demonstrate
how little is known
of each other's lives,
even those with whom we're allied.
How many hours may be missing,
hours we have no idea of,
how many more thoughts
than we thought possible
for them to think.

9.

Who is the traitor in the unclaimed land,
territory ceded
to make the boundary lines of maps
in the time other
than the time of clocks?

10.

The room is submarine,
a diving bell
on the sea floor
in international waters.
Sound comes in
muffled by the watery medium
of glass, traffic
noises radioed from far
away, even distress signals
they are in no position to answer,
having answered those
that brought them there.

11.

To win by stratagem,
to occupy another country
for some months
with its single crop.

12.

If his heart stops,
he leaves behind
the complicated disgrace
to others—
having fallen in the field,
one of the dishonored dead,
struck down
in the very act
of fleeing.

Vile

When a woman feels herself
vile—on her step out the door off
to work, or there already,
looking up from a sheaf
of papers at a steel desk—
she might be anywhere
but she must be someone
who has that in her,
not just the doing of whatever
she has done but the judging
after, and she should be
a woman without much

a priori tendency to
think of herself that way.
It's no part of the ritual
assessment of her face
at the mirror, not there in her eyes
as she lines them, or at her lips
pursed for the gloss,
or an unvoiced whisper in the whisk
of a brush through her hair,
every stroke, nothing
until now that she's become
a woman who has her reasons. Oh

don't imagine the very worst,
nobody dies, no one is ruined,
the range of the disregard's
not monstrous, but damaging
to the spirit nevertheless
already of several she loves.
The true destroyers, she has
consoled herself, have no need
of consolation, never
think of themselves as
she does with even better reasons
than she has for thinking so.

Time passes, anyway,
months pass, and the woman
begins to feel herself
less vile, for no reason
other than getting accustomed
to it, more than accustomed
she is simply tired of it,
and since she will go on—
nobody wants her not to—
having to go on
with some efficiency
seems reason enough.

THAT DREAM, YOUR DREAM, SHE SAYS

to him, where we're standing in a portico
at the top of the steps of what was
it, museum, library? You weren't sure yourself.
Light, the border we faced each other over:
one of us in shadow the other out
in sunlight, cool or warm did you say
which for whom? You did say everything
felt real—the air on the skin—the sound
the sound of me talking, saying
the words you want me to, how I will never
keep anything from you (it must have been me
in the shade, you for the light), how I
could never leave, how much what we have
is worth no matter the obstacles.
Did you truly have that dream, where you
throw your voice so that it's you,
all you at last, with me not even
there to join in my own compliance?

ENEMIES

How did they become, each to the other,
something that neither wanted to be?
No version of their lives together
exists on which they can agree.
Once taking each other for someone other
than either of them pretended to be
could nothing then change them further
than whatever changed them utterly?

Her Pleasure in Herself

At twenty-two I was instructed by
an older man, which I'm still grateful for.
Not technically a first time, first in things
that mattered, so will it qualify? All right, then.
Just out of college, I stayed around the city,
so little chance for anything back home,
but boldness for the shyest of the shy
girls I was: renting a tiny place, I worked
where I'd interned, and also waited tables.
I told myself that I was saving up
for grad school, really I was adrift and drifted
into him at my first-year roommate's wedding.
Small and intense, hands going as he talked,
witty right off how—*full vicious circle*—
he'd gone to prep school with her father here,
returned last year to teach: history,
which had been my major; his specialty,
Japan, my fascination as a child.
So we began to meet downtown for coffee;
then drinks, somewhere like this with all the booths.

More than twice my age and recently divorced,
two children grown, that everything for him
seemed afterwards, provisional, and for me
prelude, temporary, matched us I thought.
But he was wary, a disappointed man
who hadn't lost his relish just the same.
He gave in to whatever it was brought us
together, more than that, appeared to find

a purpose—needed to, I see now—something
to make us possible for him those months:
a mutuality with me as focus,
studying me so that I learned myself
with a patience that I never met again
in anyone and maybe didn't have to
because he left me so much from it, his
devotion to my coming, and removed
from any circumstance that might impede it.
Down or irritable as—I saw that look—
I am aware I can be, he had a knack
for coaxing me to bed and in bed coaxing
it out of me with those hands of his for a start,
a steady stream of touch to draw me on.
No sense of pressure for arrival: I got
there or I didn't. Most often, though, I did.
Afterwards, in keeping with the theme
of pleasing me, some talk about what had.

Sometimes I felt I loved him; sometimes not.
He didn't say too much of love himself,
something I recall about its *flickering* was
the word, against that pleasure I could count on.
A man's way, I've heard you on the subject—their
detachment—maybe that's right, but why not say
instead a healthy concentration? I learned
what pleases me, a pleasure in myself
that I could take almost no matter what,
even when not deeply or at all
in love with the one who might have given it.

Fashion Show

She'd been modeling for him
the booty of a sale: black pants
with a pattern slightly raised, iridescing
as she moved, the empire top that flowed down
over her waist—

how she looked to him! How she looked
away, shying still, even with just
the two of them, though she'd wanted so
to do this, but flitting her eyes
down from his eyes.
                              Something tentative
even in the flourish of her twirl,
near teeter on the naked foot
in strappy high heels.

The stumble was his, though,
and in mind, a sudden fall
into his black assay of everything:
childish wasn't this childish,
private showing and peek-a-boo,
childish, their collusion in her display.

But no, he righted himself,
all joys childish, versions of the earliest,
soon after self met other
and could think itself an I: I show
me to you. You see me. I see you.

PLAGUE TALE

Come lately to that place in his acquaintance
with himself, and just about to turn the corner
to the park they'll stroll, he has a sudden feeling
for things that haven't happened yet but must,
he's sure of it now,
                           and so begins to tell her
a story with intent, the one that he's
reminded of but only imperfectly
remembers, some version of a plague tale set
among the dwellers in a piney hollow,
isolates together.
                           A man, the mountainy
man of the story, bitten by something rabid
or venomous, gathers his children around him.
                                                       No,
of course he's a husband only, and it's his wife,
new wife, girl-wife, as young as she could be
up in those mountains back in that time.
                                                 He speaks
out of his fated distance to one who depends
on him but might do other than he asks,
to the beloved who must at all costs listen.
He speaks for when he'll thirst and rage, struck mad
enough to do her harm. No matter what
he says or does, threatens or begs, do not
come near, don't try to free him, leave him water,
yes, slip food into the utmost range
the chain allows his movement then run away.

What's she to do? I mean the one who hears
the telling outside the tale, and gets the warning
certainly, but still thinks he's full of it—
dopey with his notions of who depends
on whom—and what should she reply to this?

She was an English major, too. She could
go story for story with him: the fairy tale
about the little man who knows he doesn't
know a thing but picks up junk dropped in
the road—a length of rope, a chicken bone—
and by resourcefulness and pluck turns these
to tools that win for him a princess bride,
after which, finis, the narrative simply closes.

What doom has this man of hers caught anyhow?
We're all of us doomed if you think about it way
too hard, headed for what we're headed for.
She has feelings for the future of her own
that want her close by him (though not so much
when he's depressed and dire), none of which
she says by any story, few words even,
only her refusal to move off,
and right now her contrivance of a stumble
that jostles him nearly off the narrow path.

In a Breath

I liked that you couldn't forget
the beautiful thing I said
to you—pleased to be pleasing—
how when you leaned to kiss
me goodnight, just as I met
your parted lips with my lips
I had the sense I was breathing
you, could breathe you in,
could take you in like breath—
but that it could have been
so much mine, the feeling,
as to seem a solipsism
while wholly what you'd given—
was the part I left unsaid.

Mytheme

When the sight catches him,
they're in the foyer mirror entering
the house—the murmur of the party
a room away—himself, grizzled,
beside his youthful goddess,
a beauty and no question,
four years together and not a sign
of them on her—and then the fear,
its emphasis so particular in
that moment on what he might be
reduced to, not by age, but by
his literary friends, the two poets
especially, no Ovid either
one, but lovers of those ancient
patterns, professional reducers—
and never the whole story,
instead the briefest entry
in the log of small talk to index him
with Tithonus, the man who marries
Dawn, the goddess who forgets
to ask eternal youth for her beloved
when she gets him immortality.
Then he forgets, of course—Tithonus
does—repeats himself to those
whose names he blanks on, or reassigns
at random, the same old stories over
and over, told until he can't,
shrinking inward to bones gone
light as birds'—gone hair, gone teeth,
summed up in what was a metaphor
till he's become it—clack and
chirr, faint drilling in the back rooms
somewhere, the nuisance of
a cricket shut up in the house.

What Old David Felt

. . . but the King did not cohabit with her
                                        —1 Kings 1:4

For one brief moment retrograde
as Abishag came to his bed
what flared inside the aged king
was anger borne of pride that such

a man for women as he'd been
should go so docilely to sleep
beside a lovely virgin for
the temperature, that the fire burned

so low by which he once could heat
himself and others also, still
he'd do such things he knew just what
they were—and then he let it go.

Religion, Then Science

What came to him concerning lust,
a sudden thought and frightening,
was that libidinousness must
give off strong waves of energy,
a pulsing beacon that could attract
the attention of a deity
who had expressed before in lightning
displeasure as retributive act.

Later, the mental antistrophe:
person versus personified
first cause, of course that made no sense.
A different paradigm applied
surely, the nature of expense.
A universe in entropy
working bodily through him
its cool exchange: heat out, death in.

To One at Risk

The flailing semaphore of long
grass and treetops.
                    The last gap
of blue to the east closes in
an avalanche of clouds shot through
with flares,
            which root down now below
as spidering cracks, three o'clock high.

The eardrums say the world's airtight,
the darkened chamber visible
whose heavy door keeps swinging shut
after the light has opened wide.

The boom and flash converge, so you
are counting
            at the flash: one-
one-thousand, two . . .
                        and on the speed
of sound to tell you it's still far
enough away,
            on being hit
remaining so unlikely it might
as well be thought miraculous,
on having read statistics show
more people get struck twice than once,
and veteran conductors who
attract the notice of the heavens
will run in families. As must
the streak in character disdaining
shelter when the sky goes pewter
to bruise, or worse, the green into
which some have ascended bodily
upon the whirlwind.

You rush now
in pelting rain, over the meadow,
a shortcut to the insulation
of your car, up on its rubber wheels.
You think a war-room grid over
the ground, coordinates and crosshairs,
any square the one,

                   but meanwhile
you do right giving wide berth
to pole and stanchion, to the copse
of tall trees, oak grove, a single elm
and linden—

           skirting the lake, beyond
whose farther shore, downward strikes
of thin, dowser's sticks deafen
and blind.

           By feel, then, you'll discern
air gathering with premonition,
and earth, too, building up its charge
to make the coming meeting

                    you
will know you are attending by
an augural stink, oxygen
becoming ozone as the bolt
passes through air,

              and if flesh crawls
with formicate sensation, get low
to the ground, lower than it.

                    Crouch
in some concavity, as if
to abase yourself, saying *Lord,*
I mean to be no protuberance
upon the landscape,
                    if that helps,
but never prostrate. A hunker is
the position to take, still in the realm
of obeisance, in balance over the small
prints of the foot—
                    and not the press
of the entire body on the earth
of *I am nothing, I am the ground*
itself, but rather *I am a human*
being on it and I would like
to stay—there are mysteries I bow to
of which I also may be part.

This My Failure This My Life This My

Something like a mantra
comes by now unbidden,
has a little rhythm—
the idea of my failure.

Hope is it will recede,
staled by repetition,
like all other wisdom,
eventually disbelieved.

REGRET

Of all the places I have been,
I now remember most regret,
the place I've never truly been,
to which I must someday return
to see what I did not see then.

First Things

That dream of his, which throws
open all the way
certain doors and windows,
forgotten, he can start the day.

Escaped to Tell

No reason in the world for driving so
fast except you absolutely have to

get to your son in trouble in these hills—
in custody, a Southern sheriff versus

a high school boy: a rescue this is, no less,
through darkling Georgia, but what will rescue you?

The rain storms torrents into the ditches,
gouts across the windshield, sheets

over the road in the amber headlights
of the rental, pocked as beaten bronze,

and you are not exactly riding a wave
of luck yourself of late: late sister,

late brother, too early ferried over
that other river, and then your father, also.

New prisms in each eyeglass lens
do help with the persistent double vision,

but you can see the setting clearly enough.
In the wind, the tall pines blade-bend

in actual multiples, the slash of each branch,
the road's scythe-curves,

quick-lit in lightning, slicing left,
slicing right. The edge you have

against the ridiculous abundance
of bad enough and worse still,

as much as the anxious ownership
of fatherhood, to bring you through

for him and back to us, is that even
fully in the midst of everything

you're half aware of what a hell
of a story it's going to be. Is.

Passengers Will . . .

Heedless of announcement and the cabin
attendant's pantomime just in front of her,

the toddler, even her straight black hair
quivering with her clenched resistance,

will not wear the seat belt, will not
sit back in her seat to be cinched

in, her egg-oval face turned my way,
eyes wide, mouth pinched, no,

will not, as if it's a spoon
she won't take—medicine, food—a face

for refusing to know what's good
for you, hunching over till her father from

his side pries her up and her mother from hers
slips her hands in, as if to embrace,

fishing for the ends, tongue and buckle:
the fastening done and kept done

in the face of the face of tears now.
What would it be never to feel mastered,

overmastered, forced? Then the plane itself
thrusts forward and everyone back

flatly into the seats, in the throat of the gravelly
roar, and the bodiless press on all of us.

At Day's End, as at the End of Any Day

The paperback on the stone seat in the front garden,
an inadvertence so unlike him.
Among the wind-riffled pages
a thin copper bookmark
nevertheless keeps a place.

A season's worth of leaves
in the window well.

Settled inside the frosted globe of the high porch light,
wing-shred and husk
nesting the smoky black of the bulb,
and the ladder laid in the grass by the steps.

Over the foyer closet's threshold, door ajar, the sleeve
of a loden coat, slipped out
of the ranks of hangers.

The any-angled heap of papers in the middle
of the desk, and to the side,
atop a pile, a penciled list
of items on loose-leaf, with three,
four, and seven crossed out.

Three red dishes, blue mug, knife, and spoon in the sink.
A note on the refrigerator,
also out of character, *gone to sleep early.*

On the shelf by the back door with the whiny hinge,
the blaze of marigolds still in their seeds
in the sealed packet.

Evening

Such brooding on the end of day.
Day darkened; ended anyway.

Letting It in a Little

Crack the door a few inches,
and not to have your face peering

out met by a face peering in:
Janus, *volte faces*, nose to nose,

but for no one, as expected,
no polite young men,

offering the Bible as guide,
no messenger, deliverer,

nobody Nobodaddy sent
either, no one cowled, hooded,

black-suited, robed—Jesus,
what is it Halloween?

It isn't—no faceless
figure, scythe on the side,

nothing personified. Empty,
the corridor's a corridor and

adequately lit, except where
the bulb's out at the end furthest

from where you envision
the self in a small apartment behind

a hollow-core, faux colonial door.
What you'll permit access is scent,

a seepage of atmosphere, a floral
smokiness, which almost catches

in the throat and masks rot—
and sound, buzz-and-hum

of necessary motors, up-swells,
subsidences, yes, but

a thunking halt, all that
had been muffled by shutting

the door shut as tightly
as you could, relieved

to be inside. Still, you could feel
through your hand on the handle

a fumbling, and with the hand
you passed over the frame, a puffing

of draft in this drafty not-so-old
building. You can check,

though, for a person, a personage,
but it's just a breeze, not cold

yet, that's a season or two off,
a breath of air, merely, and that

whiff you'll want to allow entrance.
How can you help it? Your heart

skipped a beat in a familiar way—
medicate for it, but don't deny it—

and another beat rushed in to fill
the blank in the rhythm with double

force. Dangerous, also, it feels,
to leave the gap between the jamb

and door edge, only a silly brass
chain between—and everything

of yours at risk gets precious,
or not, and what's not is clutter

you might consider ridding yourself
of, given the prompt in the air.

That The Compensations of Art

people speak of amount to
nothing really compared to what
is taken, I shouldn't need to say.

The beloved gone, you can sing
about the beloved
being gone, if you like, praise

of the qualities
as the measure of loss.

This morning I woke
in the dark of
predawn and couldn't get

back to sleep: a twitch here, there
not quite pain, here a fear
of the boss, there a mortal
thought circling.

But also in the midst
as I was about to give up,
to turn on the lamp,
only to read, a line came to me,

which seemed to open into something,
as I followed it,
grabbed up the bedside pad

and pencil: some words, a line
of inquiry,
tracked in black, scratching
across a page
and down, wherever it led—

more words, more lines,
the sounds of
what I would say.

And no other racket
from the night-forest
of the head, and not the body sensing
itself sensing. Even fatigue,
all-purpose symptom of everything,
put by,

pages filling with huge scrawl,
turning and turning
like a calendar montage,
time passing

until that surprising version of later
arrived, the great light
having returned, drowning out
the little one of the lamp.

I half-remembered then
how light had come to the walls,
the slow dissolve into, from the first
faint tincture,

except I hadn't quite
seen it somehow, was there,
absently, elsewhere
partly, and that is what I got, the most I ever
got in exchange—
one kind of sleep for another.

SPEND, SPEND

The candles in the box bow-bend
in a heat not of their festive making,
come therefore to a useless end.
What else has wasted in the waiting?

A tangled skein of rubber bands
inside the drawer dries toward dust,
has meanwhile stuck together, and
the paper clips have finished rust.

All day the word that would elude
recall on the maddening tip of your tongue
happened to have been "desuetude."
What other words are going, have gone,

you couldn't say. You hoarded sleep
once, too, so difficult to awaken,
always of a mind to keep
what you suspect will soon be taken.

Most things you kept against the time
that didn't come you now can't find.